*God's
Promise
Kept*

MATTHEW

Book 1 *Chapters 1-16*

Marilyn Kunz

& Catherine Schell

12 Discussions for Group Bible Study

D1569214

Neighborhood Bible Studies Publishers
P.O. Box 222
56 Main Street
Dobbs, Ferry, NY 10522
1-800-369-0307
nbstudies@aol.com
www.NeighborhoodBibleStudy.org

neighborhood bible studies

GROUP PARTICIPANTS

Name	Address	Phone Number

Copyright © 1995 by Marilyn Kunz and Catherine Schell

ISBN 1-880266-18-0 (previous edition ISBN 0-8423-4188-9)
Second printing November 2002
Printed in the United States of America
Cover photo by Jiasong Zhu

CONTENTS

HOW TO USE THIS DISCUSSION GUIDE

This study guide uses the inductive approach to Bible study. *It will help you discover for yourself what the Bible says.* It will not give you prepackaged answers. *People remember most what they discover for themselves and what they express in their own words.* The study guide provides three kinds of questions:

1. What does the passage say? What are the facts?
2. What is the meaning of these facts?
3. How does this passage apply to your life?

- Observe the facts carefully before you interpret the meaning of your observations. Then apply the truths you have discovered to life today. Resist the temptation to skip the fact questions since we are not as observant as we think. Find the facts quickly so you can spend more time on their meaning and application.

- *The purpose of Bible study is not just to know more Bible truths but to apply them.* Allow these truths to make a difference in how you think and act, in your attitudes and relationships, in the quality and direction of your life.

- Each discussion requires about one hour. Decide on the amount of time to add for socializing and prayer.

- *Share the leadership.* If a different person is the moderator or question-asker each week, interest grows and members feel the group belongs to everyone. The Bible is the authority in the group, not the question-asker.

- When a group grows to more than ten, the quiet people become quieter. Plan to grow and multiply. You can meet as two groups in the same house or begin another group so that more people can participate and benefit.

TOOLS FOR AN EFFECTIVE BIBLE STUDY

1. A study guide for each person in the group.

2. A modern translation of the Bible such as:
   NEW INTERNATIONAL VERSION (NIV)
   CONTEMPORARY ENGLISH VERSION (CEV)
   JERUSALEM BIBLE (JB)
   NEW AMERICAN STANDARD BIBLE (NASB)
   REVISED ENGLISH BIBLE (REB)
   NEW REVISED STANDARD VERSION (NRSV)

3. An English dictionary.

4. A map of the Lands of the Bible in a Bible or in the study guide.

5. Your conviction that the Bible is worth studying.

GUIDELINES FOR AN EFFECTIVE STUDY

1. Stick to the passage under discussion.

2. Avoid tangents. If the subject is not addressed in the passage, put it on hold until after the study.

3. Let the Bible speak for itself. Do not quote other authorities or rewrite it to say what you want it to say.

4. Apply the passage personally and honestly.

5. Listen to one another to sharpen your insights.

6. Prepare by reading the Bible passage and thinking through the questions during the week.

7. Begin and end on time.

HELPS FOR THE QUESTION-ASKER

1. Prepare by reading the passage several times, using different translations if possible. Ask for God's help in understanding it. Consider how the questions might be answered. Observe which questions can be answered quickly and which may require more time.

2. Begin on time.

3. Lead the group in opening prayer or ask someone ahead of time to do so. Don't take anyone by surprise.

4. Ask for a different volunteer to read each Bible section. Read the question. Wait for an answer. Rephrase the question if necessary. Resist the temptation to answer the question yourself. Move to the next question. Skip questions already answered by the discussion.

5. Encourage everyone to participate. Ask the group, "What do the rest of you think?" "What else could be added?"

6. Receive all answers warmly. If needed, ask, "In which verse did you find that?" "How does that fit with verse...?"

7. If a tangent arises, ask, "Do we find the answer to that here?" Or suggest, "Let's write that down and look for the information as we go along."

8. Discourage members who are too talkative by saying, "When I read the next question, let's hear from someone who hasn't spoken yet today."

9. Use the summary questions to bring the study to a conclusion on time.

10. Close the study with prayer.

11. Decide on one person to be the host and another person to ask the questions at the next discussion.

INTRODUCTION *to the Gospel of MATTHEW*

The Gospel of Matthew was placed at the beginning of the New Testament by the early church, probably because it connects naturally with the Old Testament.

Matthew's Gospel contains most of Mark's account, compressed and rearranged to fit Matthew's design. It includes some incidents not recorded in Mark, particularly those featuring Peter. Matthew includes information about Jesus' birth not found in the other Gospels, but agrees with Luke's description as to time and place and spiritual meaning. Matthew also includes two parables not found in the other Gospels.

The early church used this Gospel widely for instruction. Matthew presents five long teaching sections by Jesus, each arranged around some central theme. Narratives of Jesus' ministry and the opposition to it separate the teaching sections. The Gospel culminates in the description of Jesus' rejection, his crucifixion, and his resurrection.

Since the first part of the second century, Matthew's name has been attached to this Gospel. It was probably written between A.D. 65 and 110, perhaps soon after the destruction of Jerusalem and its Temple in A.D. 70. Matthew wrote it in Greek, probably in a Greek-speaking area with a strong Jewish-Christian community such as Antioch in Syria, or Phoenicia on the eastern coast of the Mediterranean Sea.

The *chart* on page 76 can help you see the structure of Matthew's Gospel. Note the major divisions and how the author arranged his material. Continue to refer to this chart and fill in your own titles and notations as you study. You may refer to a *commentary* if you wish, but do not bring commentaries to the discussion.

Use the *map* on page 75 of this guide to locate places referred to in the Gospel of Matthew.

In this study guide, references to different sections of a Bible verse are indicated by letters. For instance, the first part of verse 14 is 14a, the last part is 14b.

Abbreviations of Bible versions used in this study are:
> NEW INTERNATIONAL VERSION (NIV – *all quotations are from NIV unless noted)*
> GOOD NEWS BIBLE (GNB)
> JERUSALEM BIBLE (JB)
> NEW AMERICAN STANDARD BIBLE (NASB)
> NEW ENGLISH BIBLE (REB)
> REVISED STANDARD VERSION (RSV)

DISCUSSION 1

Jesus' Birth

MATTHEW 1; 2

The Old Testament's description of the Messiah created great expectations for a king who would free the Jewish people from oppressors and establish a powerful kingdom. Matthew presents Jesus as the Messiah who would rule Israel, but with some surprises.

READ MATTHEW 1:1-17

1. Why would the three titles given to Jesus in verse 1 be important to Matthew's Jewish audience?

Note: **Christ** *is the Greek word for the Hebrew term* **Messiah**, *meaning the* **anointed one**.

2. Into what major sections does Matthew divide Jewish history?

What significant event or person closes each section?

Why do you think that Matthew includes five women when it was not the Jewish custom to include women in a genealogy?

READ MATTHEW 1:18-25

3. How does Matthew describe the circumstances surrounding the conception and birth of Jesus from Joseph's
   point of view?

4. What four things does Joseph learn in his dream?

   What impresses you about his response?

5. While Jesus' lineage is traced from Abraham to Joseph,
   Mary's husband and Jesus' legal father, how does Matthew
   emphasize the fact that Joseph is not the father of Jesus
   (verses 16, 18-21, 24, 25)?

6. According to the angel's message, what Old Testament
   prophecy is fulfilled in Jesus' birth?

7. From the meaning of the words **Jesus, Emmanuel** and
   Christ, what picture do you see of Jesus (verses 1, 21,
   23)?

READ MATTHEW 2:1-18

8. Why did the Magi make the long journey from the East?

Note: **Wise men** *or* **Magi** *were students of the stars who were able
to calculate the orbits and conjunctions of planets. One explanation of*

the star they saw is the conjunction of the planets Jupiter (star of the world ruler) and Saturn (star of Palestine) in the summer and autumn of 7 B.C.

9. What effects do the Magi's inquiries in Jerusalem have on Herod and the city (verses 3-8)?

    Why does their search for the **king of the Jews** prompt Herod to ask about where **the Christ** will be born?

10. Describe the emotions and actions of the wise men when they leave Jerusalem and when they see the child.

    What do Herod's emotions and actions reveal about his intentions (verses 8, 16)?

11. How are Herod's plans foiled?

    Imagine yourself as Joseph. What would you have felt and what would you have said to Mary during this hasty nighttime departure for Egypt?

    How are Joseph's flight to Egypt and Herod's actions part of what the Old Testament said would happen?

READ MATTHEW 2:19-23

12. Like many other powerful people, Herod used his position to exercise control over others, even to the point of destroying people to protect his own position. What perspective does verse 19a give you on the actions and value judgments of people in power?

Note: King Herod reigned from 37 to 4 B.C.

13. How does God guide Joseph to a safe location which fits into God's plan?

Why is obeying what you already know necessary before you receive further guidance?

What part does logical reasoning play in the way God guided Joseph and guides us today?

SUMMARY

1. How would you contrast Herod and Joseph in terms of: power?

resources?

motivation?

the importance of their lives?

2. In many cultures dreams play a prominent role, as they did in how God guided Joseph. What part did Joseph's obedience play in the Old Testament prophecies being fulfilled (1:21-25; 2:14, 15, 21-23)?

3. Christians struggle with keeping a balance about God's guidance. We tend to overemphasize either the intuitive, feeling-oriented ways of guidance or the totally rational intellectual approach. God has made us capable of being guided by his Spirit's using both our mind and our emotions. What do you learn about guidance and obedience from Joseph's life?

PRAYER

Lord, help me to be a Joseph in my heart—to value humility, sensitivity, faithfulness, obedience, justice, that I too may walk in your will. May you fulfill, Lord, what you want in my lifetime. Forgive me when I envy the power of the Herods of this world, even the little ones I meet along the way. Their wheeling and dealing seem so attractive when I feel unsuccessful and inadequate. They appear so clever and others seem to be impressed by them. You entrusted your servant Joseph with what looked like humble tasks; yet what an important part he had in your great plan! Help me to be a Joseph. By your grace, Amen.

CHART

Use the chart on page 76 to help you follow the chronology, locations, and major events in Matthew. After each study, write a brief title of that chapter which will help you to remember the contents.

2

Repentance and Temptation

MATTHEW 3; 4

If the King were moving to your city, how would you prepare for his arrival? If you opposed the King what methods would you use to defeat his plan? In chapter 3, Matthew moves ahead thirty years to introduce John the Baptist and the surprising sequence of events that launches Jesus' public ministry.

READ MATTHEW 3:1-6

1. In what ways does John fulfill Isaiah's prophecy in verse 3?

   He is the voice crying in the wilderness to prepare the way of the Lord

2. How are John's life and message preparing the way for the Lord?

   He was preaching about coming of Jesus. baptizing + hearing confessions.

READ MATTHEW 3:7-12

3. List the points John makes in his sermon to the Pharisees and Sadducees?

   Bear fruit + repent.
   Don't flee from wrath, but turn + repent.
   Don't lean on Abraham as ancestor.
   John baptized w/ water - but Jesus will baptize with Holy Spirit.

4. Visualizing each of John's word pictures, why do you think he uses such harsh images of judgment with these religious leaders?

In order for his words to have impact & convey the truth.

5. How does John contrast himself and his baptism with the person and actions of the one who will come after him?

water vs Holy Spirit

READ MATTHEW 3:13-17

6. How does verse 11 help explain John's reluctance to baptize Jesus?

He is not worthy to carry his sandals.

7. Why does Jesus insist on being baptized by John?

It is proper to fulfill all righteousness.

What comfort is it to you that Jesus identified with people who need to repent of their unrighteousness?

We also are unrighteousness & sinful.

8. What three things happen immediately after Jesus is baptized by John?

Heavens opened
Spirit of God descended like a dove.
God said "This is my Beloved Son."

What would these happenings say about Jesus' identity to the Jews who were familiar with Isaiah 11:2; 42:1, and Psalm 2:7?

Is. 11:2 - The spirit of the Lord shall rest upon him
42:1 - Here is my servant... in whom my soul delights.
Ps 2:7 - You are my son- today I have begotten you.

9. Remembering what has just happened in 3:16, 17, what significance do you see in the timing, the purpose, and who initiates Jesus' going into the desert?

   God had marked him as his Beloved.
   The Spirit led him into the wilderness.

10. Why would it be sin for Jesus to use his power to turn the stones into bread when he is hungry?

   one lives by every word from mouth of God

   Read the context of Jesus' answer in <u>Deuteronomy 8:1-3</u>. What insight does this give you into how Jesus views this temptation?

   God tested him, humbled him like his ancestors,
   + fed them w/ manna, to understand
   that one does not live by bread alone. but
   by God's word

11. Since we can't turn stones into bread, we don't face Jesus' temptation in those terms. However, in what area of life have you faced a similar temptation?

12. How is the second temptation (verses 5-7) different from the first one and how is it similar?

   Throw yourself down + angels will save you
   Do not put your Lord to the test

   What is Jesus' answer to the devil's use of Scripture?

13. What change of tactics in the third temptation reveals the tempter's real goal in all three temptations (verses 8-11)?

   Real goal is to have Jesus fall down +
   worship him.

14. What are the results of the way Jesus deals with the third temptation? *Away with you, Satan!*
   Worship + serve only the Lord

15. How are Jesus' replies to Satan the answer to the variety of temptations you face (verses 4, 7, 10)?

READ MATTHEW 4:12-25

16. Upon hearing of the arrest of John the Baptist, Jesus returns to Galilee but moves from Nazareth to Capernaum. What significance does Matthew see in this?

Fulfillment of Isaiah.
People in darkness have seen a great light.

17. After John can no longer preach because he is imprisoned, Jesus begins to preach. Compare their messages (3:1, 2, 8, 11, 12; 4:17).

Repent. the kingdom of heaven is near.

*Note: While **repent** comes from Greek words meaning "to change one's mind" and "to regret, to feel remorse," New Testament use of the word also involves a turning round, completely altering the basic motivation and direction of one's life.*

18. Describe the setting and Jesus' call to his first four followers (verses 18-22).

Follow me & I will make you fish for people
Simon/Peter, Andrew. James. John

Through the centuries, Christians have thought that Jesus' call to the fishermen applies to all Christians. How can you fulfill this calling?

19. Describe how you would film a short documentary of Jesus' early ministry (verses 23-25).

Check the map on page 75 for the geography involved.

SUMMARY

What impresses you the most about Jesus at the beginning of his public ministry?

PRAYER

Lord Jesus, Son of God, we know little about the pressure of temptation because we seldom resist long enough to discover what it means. Help us to heed your call to repent, to change our minds about what is important in life, about who deserves our loyalty. Help us to leave all other loyalties and follow you. For your name's sake, Amen.

CHART

In the chart on page 76, what title can you write for these chapters that will help you remember their main points?

DISCUSSION 3

Teaching on a Mountain

MATTHEW 5

If you heard both John the Baptist and Jesus preach, ***"Repent, for the kingdom of heaven is near,"*** what questions would you want to ask? What and where is the kingdom of heaven? How do I get in? How is it different from the kingdom I'm in now?

As large crowds flock to Jesus, he withdraws to a quiet place. In the Sermon on the Mount, chapters 5-7, Jesus teaches his disciples about the kingdom of God and the characteristics of people in God's kingdom.

READ MATTHEW 5:1-12

1. Read 4:24, 25 in connection with 5:1. What seems to be Jesus' motive in choosing this time and place to teach?

Note: ***He sat down***—*the traditional way for rabbis to teach.*

2. What pattern do you observe in what Jesus says in this section?

3. Read verses 3-11 again, reading ***happy*** (GNB) for ***blessed***. What qualities and values are important to Jesus?

In what ways do Jesus' teachings turn the generally accepted values of your society upside down?

4. What examples of these desired qualities have you seen in a person's life?

    Which ones do you desire most for yourself?

5. What are the two reasons Jesus' disciples have for being glad about any undeserved persecution?

    Theirs is the kingdom of Heaven
    Their reward is great in Heaven

    Since the time Jesus said these words, many men and women around the world have suffered for doing right and for being his followers. What level of persecution do you observe against Christians today?

READ MATTHEW 5:13–16

6. Jesus describes his followers as salt and light. List as many uses for salt as you can.

    What use can you think of for salt that has lost its saltiness?

    As *the salt of the earth*, what quality of life and functions are the disciples of Jesus to have?

7. As a clearly visible city on a hill or a lighted lamp in a house, what effect does Jesus expect his followers to have on the world around them?

Let their light shine to give glory to God.

Suggest ways in which you can **let your light shine before men** today so that they will praise your Father in heaven.

READ MATTHEW 5:17-20

8. What is Jesus' attitude and intention concerning the Old Testament law and the prophets?

He has come not to abolish, but to fulfill.

Trace what Matthew has said about the **king** and the **kingdom of heaven**: 2:2, 6; 3:1, 2; 4:17; 5:3, 10, 19, 20.

9. What is the relationship between obedience and greatness in the kingdom of heaven?

Whoever breaks commandments will be least – whoever does them will be great

How can your righteousness surpass the righteousness of the Pharisees who kept all the laws meticulously?

READ MATTHEW 5:21-48

10. What pattern do you observe repeated in verses 21, 22; 27, 28; 31, 32; 33, 34; 38, 39; 43, 44?

11. Jesus discusses six issues from the law. In each case, how do Jesus' requirements differ from the scribes and Pharisees' interpretations of the law to which he refers in verse 20?

12. What effects do your relationships with other people have on your relationship with God the Father (verses 23, 24)?

13. Unresolved anger, lustful thoughts, easy divorce, dishonest speech, a "get even" attitude toward one's enemies—all continue to be relevant issues. Ask each person in your group to take a different one of these problems and apply Jesus' advice to such a situation today.

14. How is our *heavenly Father* a model of the behavior Jesus urges that we exercise toward our enemies as well as our friends?

SUMMARY

1. Imagine that you are hearing the message of Jesus in this chapter for the first time. What are your impressions?

What are your reactions?

2. How do Jesus' teachings in verses 21-48 illustrate his purpose to *fulfill the law and the prophets* (verse 17)?

3. What connection do you see between the qualities of character of those who belong to the kingdom of heaven (verses 3-12) and the attitudes and actions Jesus commands in verses 21-48?

PRAYER

Lord, how did your first followers hear this message? Did their hearts leap with joy in recognizing the eternal truth of your teaching? Did their minds whirl as they sensed the practical implications of what you require? Were many saying, "Yes, but Lord . .."? Free us, Lord Jesus, to plunge ahead into what you call us to be and to do. We want to be salt and light in the communities where we live. For your glory, Amen.

CHART

How will you title this chapter on the chart on page 76?

DISCUSSION 4

Religion: Ritual or Reality

MATTHEW 6; 7

In the kingdom of God, how do you pray, give your offerings, face worry and insecurity, demonstrate righteousness? Where do you get your rewards? How do you know what pleases God?

As he completes his Sermon on the Mount, Jesus answers these questions. He warns against religious practices done for the wrong motive, and continues to explain life in God's righteous kingdom.

READ MATTHEW 6:1-18

1. How is Jesus' command in verse 1 an introduction to this whole section?

2. What motivations does Jesus attack in the matter of giving to the needy (verses 1-4)?

   What better way does Jesus suggest?

   How do you think that the rewards mentioned in verses 2 and 4 differ?

3. If Jesus were giving this sermon to you, would he need to begin by emphasizing the need and responsibility to give, before getting to the motives and methods of giving?

4. What are we *not* to do in prayer and why (verses 5-8)?

   What wrong ideas about God and prayer does Jesus correct?

5. If our heavenly Father knows what we need before we ask him, why do we so frequently start our prayers by telling him our problems and needs?

6. Analyze the prayer Jesus gives his disciples (verses 9-13) in terms of:
   the major requests

   the order in which they appear

   the areas they cover

7. What is Jesus' teaching on forgiveness in verses 14, 15?

   Why are some people apparently unable to receive the forgiveness the Lord would like them to have?

8. What pattern does Jesus repeat in dealing with fasting (verses 16-18)?

9. Jesus presents two types of "religious" rewards in verses 1-18. How can you obtain the kind you really want?

READ MATTHEW 6:19-24

10. What value judgments is Jesus asking his disciples to make?

11. How can you work out the tension between treasures on earth and treasures in heaven?

*Note: In Jewish thought a **sound eye** or **good eye** was a generous disposition; a **bad eye** was a covetous or stingy disposition.*

READ MATTHEW 6:25-34

12. Find at least five reasons Jesus gives for his followers not to be anxious.

How do you relate to each of these reasons?

13. Jesus gives his antidote for anxiety in verse 33. Looking at his teachings in 5:21 to 6:24, how well are you doing in seeking God's kingdom and righteousness?

14. What reasons does Jesus give for his commands in:

verses 1-5?

verse 6?

verses 7-12?

verses 13-14?

verses 15-23?

15. How would you describe in brief phrases the things against which Jesus warns us?

READ MATTHEW 7:24-29

16. What warning and promise does Jesus give in concluding his sermon?

By what criteria does the Lord judge those who claim to be members of his kingdom (verses 16, 20, 21, 24)?

17. How have you seen a storm in life reveal a person's real foundation?

SUMMARY

1. What dangers in religious practices does this study help you to avoid?

2. Which part of Jesus' teaching in chapters 6 and 7 is most appropriate for your situation today?

PRAYER

Our Father in heaven, may your name be held holy, your kingdom come, your will be done on earth as it is in heaven. Give us today the food we need; and forgive us the wrong we have done, as we have forgiven those who have wronged us. And do not put us to the test, but save us from the evil one. Through Jesus Christ our Lord. [*]

CHART

How will you title these chapters on the chart on page 76?

[*]Matthew 6:9-13, JB, NEB, NIV.

DISCUSSION 5

Miracles

MATTHEW 8; 9

Some motivational speakers today draw large crowds in spite of the high cost of admission. Their books make the top ten list. Their voice of authority and their solutions to problems captivate their audience. But how do they respond to desperate people in impossible situations? How do they react to their critics or to devoted followers?

After Jesus' long teaching session (chapters 5-7), he walks through the villages, meeting needy people from every social class. He arouses controversy and opposition as he reveals his wide range of power.

READ MATTHEW 8:1-17

1. What do you know about the leper from what he does and says (verses 1-4)?

   What would it mean to the leper for Jesus to heal him by touching him?

   Why do you think Jesus instructs him as he does?

2. List at least five things you observe about the centurion (verses 5–13).

Note: The centurion, a soldier of the Roman army commanded 100 men. He was a Gentile.

Why is Jesus astonished by the man?

3. What warning does Jesus give to his Jewish listeners?

4. What significance does Matthew see in the events of the day that Jesus goes to Peter's house (verses 14–17)?

5. What impresses you about the way Jesus responds to the diverse people who come to him for help (verses 1–17)?

READ MATTHEW 8:18-22

6. What insights do these two conversations give you into how people respond to Jesus, and the different ways he responds to them?

Compare verse 21 with 10:37.

7. Why does a person need to count the cost before deciding to follow Jesus?

READ MATTHEW 8:23-27

8. Remember that at least four of Jesus' disciples are fishermen. What does this suggest about the severity of the storm and the confidence they have in Jesus?

What tone of voice and emphasis do you think Jesus uses in verse 26?

9. What do the disciples learn about Jesus and about themselves from this frightening experience?

READ MATTHEW 8:28-34

10. If you had been one of the pig herders, how would you describe to the pigs' owners what happened?

11. Why do the townspeople ask Jesus to leave the area?

In what situations are you tempted today to make your business (pigs) more important than people?

READ MATTHEW 9:1-17

12. Jesus' actions provoke opposition and questions. In each of these three incidents, what issue do people raise and how does Jesus respond (verses 1-8; 9-13; 14-17)?

What new claim does Jesus make, and how does he prove it (verses 1-8)?

13. Why can't the *old* (forms, patterns, customs) contain the *new* that Jesus is bringing (verses 16, 17, and 14)?

READ MATTHEW 9:18-34

14. Describe the part that faith plays in what happens to the synagogue ruler's daughter, the woman, and the two blind men.

How does the ruler express his faith, and the woman her faith?

How does Jesus challenge the faith of the two blind men?

15. What reasons do you see for each negative response to Jesus in verses 24, 31, 34?

READ MATTHEW 9:35-38

16. In this summary paragraph what impresses you about Jesus' ministry, his attitude toward people, and his priorities?

SUMMARY

1. Which incident in Chapters 8 and 9 is most meaningful to you? Why?

2. Adding the events of Chapters 8 and 9 to Jesus' teachings in Chapters 5-7, what overall picture do you get of Jesus?

PRAYER

Lord, you challenged the Pharisees to learn the meaning of the Old Testament words, **I desire mercy, not sacrifice.** *You want us to care about the needs of others rather than merely performing religious duties. Thank you for showing us in these chapters what mercy is. Help us to be merciful! Amen.*

CHART

What titles can you give to these chapters on the chart on page 76?

DISCUSSION 6

Lessons in Discipleship

MATTHEW 10

W hat kind of pep talk would a company president give to his sales force before sending them out for the first time? Would he emphasize the dangers to avoid, the clever gimmicks to use, the appealing rewards for success?

At this point in Jesus' ministry the disciples' role begins to change. They move from observers to active participants. Jesus prepares them to take responsibility and face the repercussions.

READ MATTHEW 10:1-4

1. What connection do you see between Jesus' concern for the crowds and his enlistment of the twelve (9:35-10:4)?

   Between his authority and that of the twelve?

2. What special notations are made about various disciples?

Note: The Zealots were a political group opposed to paying taxes to Rome or calling any man a king. As strong nationalists they would avoid all contact with Jews who cooperated with Rome.

3. What does Jesus instruct the twelve to do and not to do (verses 5 -14)?

What do the instructions regarding travel money and luggage add up to (verses 8b-10)?

4. Why do the disciples need these instructions for handling acceptance and rejection (verses 11-15)?

Note: Sodom and Gomorrah were such wicked cities that God totally destroyed them (Genesis 13:13; 19:24, 25).

5. How do you imagine the disciples feel when Jesus tells them what they are to expect from men (verses 16-23)?

What does it mean to be like *sheep in the midst of wolves*[*], *wise as serpents*[*], and *innocent as doves*?

[*]RSV

6. Why and how will the political leaders and Gentiles hear Jesus' message (verses 17-20)?

7. If disciples are put on trial *on Jesus' account*, what may they expect from God?

8. How would knowing that Jesus' truth might divide your family prepare you to stand firm (verses 21, 22)?

9. Jesus commands standing firm to the end (verse 22) and also fleeing persecution (verse 23). Describe how both of these commands could apply in a situation today.

*Note: Scholars express various opinions on the meaning of "**You will not finish going through all the cities of Israel, before the Son of Man comes**" (verse 23). It may refer to Christ's coming in judgment in the destruction of Jerusalem and its Temple in A.D. 70, or perhaps to his coming in the power of his resurrection (Matthew 28:18-20).*

READ MATTHEW 10:24-33

10. Why should Jesus' followers then and today expect to be treated as Jesus was?

Note: **Beelzebub** *(verse 25b) is the* **prince of demons** *(9:32-34).*

11. Why are Jesus' disciples not to be afraid and to pro-claim his message boldly in the difficult situations described (verses 26-31)?

How do Jesus' warnings and promises affect your fears?

12. In what ways are you tempted to deny or disown Jesus today (verses 32, 33)?

READ MATTHEW 10:34-42

13. Why may the complete allegiance Jesus calls for in verses 32, 33 disturb family peace?

14. What makes one *worthy* of Jesus (verses 37-39)?

What does it mean to *find* or *lose* your life (verse 39)?

What difference does it make *how* one *loses his life*?

Note: In Jesus' day, to take one's cross meant literally to prepare to die by crucifixion.

15. In Matthew 6:1-18 Jesus talked about actions that God rewards. What new insights does he give about rewards in verses 40-42?

16. Why do you think that even the smallest help given to those who serve the Lord is rewarded?

What opportunities do you have to receive and to help those serving Jesus?

Summary

1. If you were one of the twelve disciples, how would you feel about the instructions you have been given?

   What would you understand to be your job description?

2. What words of comfort would you hold on to?

Prayer

Lord, when the apostles heard all your instructions and warnings, did some of them want to put in for early retirement? Your message doesn't sound like the success-oriented sales pitch for Christians we hear some places today. Lord Jesus, grant those who truly desire to serve you the courage and the endurance and the commitment it takes to be worthy of you. For your name's sake, Amen.

Chart

Write a title for this chapter that will help you remember the main points.

Questions, Fulfillment, and Invitation

MATTHEW 11

After Jesus explains the responsibilities, costs and rewards of being his disciple (chapter 10), you might ask, "Who qualifies?" Is there any place for people with questions, for the weary, for children, for ordinary people?

As Jesus teaches in the cities of Galilee, he welcomes questions from his friend, John the Baptist. He warns his opponents. He extends God's loving invitation to those who least expect it.

READ MATTHEW 11:1-6

1. John predicted that the One coming after him would bring judgment (3:11, 12). Why may John wonder from the reports of Jesus' ministry, if Jesus really is who John has thought him to be?

Note: John the Baptist was arrested because he told King Herod that it was wrong for Herod to take his brother's wife. (14:3,4).

2. Compare Jesus' reply with Old Testament passages John would have known, Isaiah 35:5, 6; 61:1. How does this answer John's question?

3. How does verse 6 apply to John, or disciples today whose circumstances may cause them to doubt Jesus?

READ MATTHEW 11:7-19

4. What point is Jesus making by the series of questions he addresses to the crowd about John (verses 7-9)?

5. What Old Testament prophecies has John fulfilled (verses 10-14; Malachi 3:1; 4:5, 6)?

What important role has John played in relation to the era of the Prophets and the Law now ending (5:17) and in relation to the era of the kingdom of heaven now beginning (4:17)?

6. In spite of John's important work, why are even the **least in the kingdom of heaven greater** (more privileged) **than he** (verse 11)?

7. In what ways has the people's response to Jesus and to John the Baptist been like that of petulant children who cannot be pleased?

8. What excuses do people offer today for a negative response to the gospel message, no matter which way it is presented to them?

READ MATTHEW 11:20-24

9. Which cities does Jesus especially criticize and why?

How does he compare their opportunities (4:23, 24; 8:5-16) with those which Tyre and Sidon and Sodom had in Old Testament days?

10. What does it mean to *repent* (verse 20)?

Note: **Repent** *was the message of John the Baptist (3:1) and of Jesus (4:17).*

What is the warning for people who learn of Jesus' power and message but refuse to repent?

READ MATTHEW 11:25-30

11. If you were arranging a musical background for this chapter, how would you indicate the change between verses 20-24 and this section?

12. From Jesus' prayer, what insight do you get into the attitudes of the people of Korazin, Bethsaida, and Capernaum who didn't accept Jesus' message and ministry?

13. From verses 25-27, what do you learn about the relationship between Jesus and the Father? Compare John 1:18.

14. How does one come to know the Lord of heaven and earth (verses 25-27)?

15. Whom does Jesus invite and what does he promise?

Note: **"Take my yoke upon you"** *means, "Enroll yourselves as my disciples."*

What is the connection between the character of Jesus and the kind of yoke he offers?

16. How would you explain what is God's part and what is your part in knowing God and finding rest for your soul (verses 27-30)?

How have you found Jesus' promises in verses 28-30 to be true in your life?

SUMMARY

1. In this chapter, in what different ways were Jesus' claims received by:
John the Baptist

the crowds

Korazin, Bethsaida, Capernaum

the wise and learned

little children

the weary and burdened

2. With which response do you most identify?

PRAYER

Lord Jesus, you make it possible for me to know the Father. I don't have to know everything or be mature in my understanding. I don't have to be on top of life or "have it all together." I can be ignorant of great theological issues. I can be overburdened by life, even a failure, and I can come to you for rest of soul. I can come to you for a safe place, a yoke that fits me, an acceptable burden. Thank you, Lord Jesus. Amen.

CHART

What title will you give this chapter to help you remember its contents?

DISCUSSION 8

Accusations and Claims

MATTHEW 12

W hich are more important, people or rules? How can you decide in a specific situation?

The clash between the Pharisees and Jesus over this issue escalates their alienation. Jesus meets their hostility with astounding claims about himself. In this emotionally charged environment Jesus responds to his enemies, his friends, and the uncommitted.

READ MATTHEW 12:1–14

1. The Pharisees as well as Jesus' disciples are following him around Galilee. Why do the Pharisees criticize the disciples for eating grain when they are hungry?

Note: According to Jewish law, it was lawful to pick grain with your hands when passing a neighbor's field (Deuteronomy 23:25).

2. What point is Jesus making by the two illustrations he uses to answer their accusation (verses 3–5)?

Note: 1 Samuel 21:1–6; Numbers 28:9, 10, are the Old Testament passages Jesus uses.

3. What two claims does Jesus make about himself in this situation (verses 6-8)?

4. What mistake do the Pharisees make because they fail to understand that God desires mercy, not sacrifice (verse 7; 9:10-13; Hosea 6:6)?

5. Describe at least one present-day instance in which you or people you know have put inappropriate emphasis on legalistic issues and missed the heart of the matter.

6. What motivates those in the synagogue who question Jesus (verses 9, 10)?

How does Jesus answer by argument and by action?

7. What do the Pharisees reveal about their value system regarding property and people (verses 9-14)?

In what way may some of us today be as guilty of inappropriate value judgments?

READ MATTHEW 12:15-21

8. What new fulfillment of prophecy does Matthew see in Jesus' withdrawal from the plotting Pharisees in the synagogue?

9. How do Jesus' actions and words fit the description of God's servant?

READ MATTHEW 12:22-37

10. Describe the two reactions to Jesus' healing of the blind and mute, demon-possessed man (verses 22-24).

*Note: The Jews believed that the Messiah would be from the line of David, **the Son of David**.*

11. Think through the four answers Jesus gives the Pharisees (verses 25-29). What should his reasoning lead them to conclude about the source and degree of his power?

12. Put Jesus' statement in verse 30 into your own words.

Why is neutrality about Jesus not an option?

13. Read verses 24, 28, 31, 32 in sequence. What are the Pharisees in danger of doing by attributing to Beelzebub the power of the Holy Spirit shown in healing the blind and mute, demon-possessed man?

14. How have the Pharisees' words condemned them?

Why do you think God is so interested in our words?

READ MATTHEW 12:38-45

15. The Pharisees have seen Jesus heal the blind and mute, demon-possessed man (verse 22) and admitted that Jesus cast out demons (verse 24). Still they challenge Jesus to give them a miraculous sign. How does he answer them?

Note: ***Adulterous*** *refers to their unfaithfulness to God.*

16. How are Jesus' hearers failing to follow the good example of the people of Nineveh or the Queen of the South?

17. What warning does Jesus give the Pharisees and scribes in the parable he tells (verses 43-45)?

READ MATTHEW 12:46-50

18. What lesson does Jesus teach about his true family?

How can you evaluate if you meet Jesus' requirement as his disciples in the crowd did?

SUMMARY

1. What contrasts would you draw between Jesus and his opponents in their attitudes and actions throughout this chapter?

2. From Jesus' claims in this chapter, what new insight or appreciation do you have of him and his ministry?

verse 6

verse 8

verses 41, 42

verses 49, 50

PRAYER

Lord Jesus, you make it very hard. You hold each of us responsible for the way we respond to everything in life—how we judge, how we react, what we value, what we decide about you, what we do about what we hear and see. It's so easy to be like the Pharisees, refusing to see the truth when it disagrees with our preconceived ideas. Help us to love mercy more than sacrifice, to think before we react, to realize what it will mean to give account on the day of judgment. Forgive us, Lord, and help us. Amen.

CHART

Write a title on the chart that summarizes this chapter.

DISCUSSION 9

Parables of the Kingdom

MATTHEW 13

*R*ead the instructions before you start to assemble this product. Good advice, but often the pictures and diagrams help more than the words. The more difficult or abstract the ideas, the more we need illustrations. As a master teacher, Jesus knew this principle.

Jesus speaks to the crowd in parables, pictures from ordinary life that illustrate spiritual truth. His audience could remember and understand the stories more than abstract points. After the crowd leaves, Jesus explains the parables at the disciples' request.

READ MATTHEW 13:1-23

1. Jesus moves from a home to the seaside to accommodate the crowds and use the water as a natural amplifier. In the first parable that Jesus tells, what are the four places the seeds fall, and what happens to the seed in each case (verses 3-8)?

   How would you have reacted if you had heard Jesus' command in verse 9 after the parable?

2. What reasons does Jesus give his disciples for teaching in parables (verses 10-17)?

3. In what way does God's evaluation of Isaiah's audience describe many who have come to hear Jesus (verses 14, 15)?

4. In what sense do verses 16, 17 describe Jesus' disciples today as well as then?

5. What are the seed, soils, fruit, in Jesus' explanation of the parable of the sower (verses 18-23)?

6. Give current examples of the things that hinder personal spiritual growth and fruit-bearing.

verse 19

verses 20, 21

verse 22

How have you learned to develop *roots* and free yourself from the *deceitfulness of wealth?*

7. Why do you think there are differences in the crop even in the good soil, the people who **hear** and **understand** the word (verse 23)?

weds 12/15/10

READ MATTHEW 13:24-43

8. Why doesn't the owner of the field follow the suggestion of his servants (verses 24-30)?
    Fearful of uprooting wheat along with weeds

    What is his major concern?
    Let all grow until the harvest

9. In the parables of the mustard seed and the yeast, what does Jesus teach about the expected growth and influence of the kingdom of heaven (verses 31-33)?
    Small beginning can result in huge ending. Faith moves mountains

Note: Matthew sees this teaching in parables as another fulfillment of Old Testament prophecy, this time from Psalm 78:2.

10. In response to his disciples' request for an explanation of the parable of the weeds, how does Jesus identify the various parts of the parable (verses 36-43)? *weeds - children of evil one*
    sower - Son of Man
    field - world
    good seed - children of kingdom

    enemy sower - Satan
    harvest - end of age
    reapers - angels

    Describe the great contrast between the ultimate fate of **the sons of the kingdom** and **the sons of the evil one**.
    sons of kingdom - shine
    sons of evil - burn

11. What does this parable teach about God's patience and our accountability?

12. What do the first two parables reveal about the value of the kingdom of heaven, and how you may encounter it (verses 44–46)?

   What does it mean to sell all that one has to *buy* the kingdom of heaven?

   How would you estimate what value you place on the kingdom of heaven?

13. How is the parable of the net (verses 47–50) similar to and different from the parable of the weeds?

14. Why is Jesus concerned that his disciples then and now understand the parables (verses 51, 52)?

READ MATTHEW 13:53-58

15. When Jesus teaches in his home town synagogue, what is the essence of the people's questions about him?

   Why is assuming you know all there is to know about Jesus dangerous, then or now?

16. Because of their *lack of faith*, Jesus did not do many miracles there. How may unbelief on our part limit what Jesus is able to do in and through us?

SUMMARY

1. If Jesus were teaching here today, do you think he would put so much emphasis on hearing and understanding? Why, or why not?

2. What most impresses you from all that Jesus says here about the *kingdom of heaven*? Why?

PRAYER

Thank you, Lord, for the privilege of seeing you through the testimony of Matthew, and of hearing your words to us. Thank you for this opportunity to study your word. Make us conscious of the importance of being good soil, not letting ourselves be distracted by daily pressures or concern about success and living the good life. Don't let unbelief keep us from having your best for us. Amen.

CHART

What title for the chart will help you remember this chapter?

DISCUSSION 10

Miracles in Gentile Territory

[handwritten: Herod Antipas son of Herod the Great - kill Jesus as baby HA sent JC to Pontius for execution]

MATTHEW 14

If you're ever tempted to be controlled by what others think of you, you can identify with Herod at his birthday party. If you have ever needed a day of solitude but found your favorite spot over run with children on a field trip, you can identify with Jesus as he steps out of the boat. If you have ever taken a risk and failed, you can identify with Peter as he cries for help.

Watch how Jesus handles an interruption of his plans, his disappointed and frightened disciples, and those who touch him in faith.

READ MATTHEW 14:1-12

1. How does Herod react to the news about the miracles of Jesus? *[handwritten: worried that John the Baptist had come back to life. Fearful & guilty about putti]*

Note: Although John was killed earlier, Matthew inserts that information here.

What have you observed about the operations of a guilty conscience? *[handwritten: prompts one to be furtive, secretive fearful]*

2. Describe the events surrounding the death of John the Baptist. Why was John imprisoned in the first place, and why later killed? *John spoke the truth about Herod's unlawful marriage to his niece - Herodias - wife of his brother. Imprisoned in fortress of Machoerus*

3. In what situations is it easy for you to be governed by what other people will think? *new/unfamiliar*

Baptism of Jesus end of John's ministry

READ MATTHEW 14:13-21

4. ***When Jesus heard*** about King Herod's thinking he was John the Baptist, why would he want to be alone? *Fearful of Herod's persecution - imprisonment or beheading - Also to grieve over John's death*

Note: ***What had happened***, verse 13, refers to verses 1, 2, before the flashback about John's death. *The northern end of the lake was outside Herod's territory*.

5. How are Jesus' plans for a quiet withdrawal disrupted? *People came out of the cities & followed him on foot*

   How does he react to what he sees? *with compassion healed the sick   transform his own sadness over John to sadness for those in need*

   How can you learn to handle interruptions of your plans with compassion?

6. Put yourself in the place of one of the disciples and trace your emotions through each step of this event (verses 15-21).

As you pick up the twelve baskets of leftovers from five loaves of bread, what would you be thinking and feeling?

READ MATTHEW 14:22-27

12 baskets -
12 tribes of Israel
Jesus feeding in wilderness = new Moses

7. In John's account of the feeding of the 5,000, he adds that the people intended to **make** Jesus **king by force** (John 6:14, 15). How does that reaction to the miracles explain Jesus' sending the disciples away immediately (verse 22)?

8. Considering the intent of the crowd, what pressures and temptation may Jesus face? *to become powerful as king over all*

Review the three temptations in Matthew 4:3-10.

9. While Jesus is praying, what is happening to the disciples? *storm comes up*

Note: *The fourth watch is between 3:00 and 6:00 A.M.*

Imagine their conversation and thoughts after the events of this long day and now the storm.

Imagine their thoughts and feelings when they see Jesus on the lake. *they were afraid he was a spirit*

10. How do Jesus' words, **"Take courage! It is I. Don't be afraid"**, comfort his disciples then and now?

READ MATTHEW 14:28-36

11. How would you characterize Peter's response to *"It is I, don't be afraid"* (verses 28-31)?

still skeptical, faith mixed w/ doubt & fear acts w/out thinking

What do you learn from Peter about taking risks by faith?

What do you learn about Jesus from his response to Peter (verses 29-31)?

knew he doubted tried to reassure him - come saves him when he falls gently rebukes him for doubt

He asks us to do the impossible.

12. Why do you think this event prompts the disciples in the boat to respond as they do in verses 32, 33?

another example of J's miraculous works.

13. How do you account for the way Jesus is greeted at Gennesaret (verses 34-36; 9:20-22)?

How has a friend's story of what Jesus did for her or him, encouraged you to bring your need to Jesus?

SUMMARY

If you were a reporter for the *Galilee Times,* what picture would you try to give of Jesus as you describe the events in this study?

PRAYER

Lord, it seems I'm always getting in over my head, like Peter. I have to cry out again and again, "Lord, save me!" Save me from my rash acts; save me from my selfish motives, my lack of faith. Save me from failure to see the needs of others, and from my lack of compassion. Amen.

CHART

What title will you give chapter 14 on the chart on page 76 to help you remember its contents?

DISCUSSION

11

Clean and Unclean; More Miracles

MATTHEW 15

*O*ne *rotten apple spoils the whole barrel. Birds of a feather flock together.* Parents use such proverbs to warn their children about the company they keep. They recognize that associating with a group or individual can lead to taking on their bad attitudes and actions. The Pharisees went far beyond this. They thought that even a momentary physical touch by a Gentile caused spiritual contamination and required cleansing by ceremonial washings.

In this study, the Pharisees confront Jesus over this issue. By his teaching and his actions, Jesus gives us a new view of what makes a person clean or unclean.

READ MATTHEW 15:1-9

1. This religious delegation comes 70 miles from Jerusalem to question Jesus about his disciples' behavior. How does Jesus focus on the real issues involved (verses 1-6)?

Note: This is a question of ritual cleansing, not of hygiene. Tradition said one could become ceremonially unclean by touching even the dust where a Gentile had stepped.

2. How does Jesus illustrate one way the Pharisees break the **command of God**?

   whatever I have to help you has been given to God

   See Exodus 20:12; 21:17 for the command.

*Note: The practice allowed the owner to enjoy the benefits of the designated money or property while he lived, but he could not use them for anything or anyone else. It was **devoted to God**, to the religious establishment.*

3. What practices of many cults today are comparable, particularly regarding honoring parents?

4. How can you use the two tests Jesus gives in verses 6 and 8 to evaluate your religious traditions?

   Do we invalidate word of God for sake of tradition, or profit? Do we walk the walk, not just talk the talk

5. Describe any traditions from your own church or denomination which you think may violate the intent of God's law. *supporting tradition against innovation*

6. Jesus concludes his confrontation with the Pharisees and scribes from Jerusalem by quoting Isaiah 29:13 to define their hypocrisy. How could you rewrite the quotation to become a description of true religion?

   hypocrite - someone who puts on a mask to play a part.

   These people honor me with their lips, not with their heart

7. What connection do you observe between what Jesus teaches the crowd (verses 10, 11) and the confrontation he has just had with the Pharisees and scribes?

what comes out of mouth defiles man
P. teach human lessons - worship w/ lips
lip-service

8. What does Jesus say about the Pharisees by the two illustrations he uses in verses 13, 14?

uprooted
blind- leading blind

9. Again the disciples receive an explanation of the parable because they *ask* for it. According to Jesus *what is not* the source of defilement, and *what is?*

evil thoughts + actions defile
not eating w/ unclean hands

How does this differ from the Pharisees' teaching (verses 2, 20)?

10. What is the difference between the first thing listed in verse 19 and the remainder of the list?

thought vs action

11. If a microphone were put near your mouth, what would an analysis of a twenty-four hour tape recording reveal about the condition of your heart?

12. On the map on page 75 trace the distance between Gennesaret (14:34) on the Sea of Galilee and the region of Tyre and Sidon (15:21), Gentile territory.

13. Have the group do a radio-style dramatization of the events described in verses 22-28.

14. What do you learn about the Canaanite woman from this incident?

recognizes Jesus as Lord
persistent

How does this woman express her faith at each point?

worships him
calls him Lord

*Note: The Greek verb used for **send her away** means let her go with her request granted.*

15. What do you learn about Jesus from this encounter?

In what ways does Jesus reward her faith?

heals her daughter
honors her great faith

How does this encourage you to bring your needs to Jesus even if you feel like an outsider or unworthy?

READ MATTHEW 15:29-39

16. Jesus' travels, lasting several weeks or longer, and the events in verses 21-39, take place in predominantly Gentile territory. How do the Gentiles respond to Jesus' acts of mercy (verses 29-31)?

came to him w/ sick
glorifying God of Israel
amazed at miracles
Jesus fulfilling old prophesies (Isaiah 35, 5-6)

17. Compare this incident with the feeding of the 5,000 in 14:13-21.

[margin handwriting: great ... many - any ... gentiles ... recognized ... Jesus as ... Messiah ... while ... people of ... Judah ... failed to]

In what details are they different and in what ways similar? *5,000* *5 loaves 12 fishes* *4,000* *gave thanks, gave to disciples*
solitary place. gave thanks. 12 baskets left over *on mt. 7 loaves few fishes. J. got on ship 7 bask*

Note: The baskets mentioned in the feeding of the 5,000 were small baskets frequently carried by Jews. The baskets in the feeding of the 4,000 in primarily Gentile territory were large hampers used by Gentiles.

SUMMARY

1. Jesus does not set out to have a ministry among the Gentiles, people the Pharisees considered unclean. Nevertheless, what do they receive from him and why?

2. What impresses you the most in Jesus' teaching about defilement (verses 10-20)?

PRAYER

"Lord, have mercy on me. Lord, help me!" I'm thankful, Lord Jesus, that you heard the prayer of that Canaanite Gentile woman. I'm so glad you took her seriously, that you honored her persistent faith. Thank you for including the Gentiles in your compassion, then and now. Thank you for making a way for our hearts to become clean. Amen.

CHART

What title can you give this chapter to remember it by?

DISCUSSION 12

"You Are the Christ, the Son of the Living God"

MATTHEW 16

How do students feel about taking midterm exams? You gather information, do experiments, discuss possible points of view, and then the test comes. You have to commit yourself to an answer. Often only when the teacher returns your test paper are you sure that you got it right.

The disciples have watched and listened to Jesus for three years in all kinds of settings. They have preached and healed with his authority. Now Jesus takes them to a remote spot for the midterm exam. His response to their answers and his next assignment startle disciples in every generation.

READ MATTHEW 16:1-4

men given to archive Word of God

1. As soon as Jesus returns from his journey into Gentile territory, the Pharisees and Sadducees ask him for a sign. What do you think they hope to see?

    his failure or a real miracle?

    How do you think they would have responded to such a sign? *disbelief scorn*

2. Why does Jesus refuse to give them what they ask?
    sees them as hypocrites wicked + adulterous generation

Compare verse 4 with 12:38-41.

*Note: The **Pharisees** were a religious party in Judaism, strict in obeying the law of Moses and the multitude of regulations added to it through the centuries. The **Sadducees** were a smaller religious party, composed mostly of priests. Their beliefs, based mainly on the first five books of Moses in the Old Testament, differed in a number of ways from the beliefs and practices of the Pharisees.*

READ MATTHEW 16:5-12

3. What insight do you get into the daily life of Jesus and the disciples from verse 5? Matthew doesn't tell us whose job it was that day to bring provisions, or how often this sort of thing happened as they traveled.

   worried little bunch; more concerned w/ stomachs than w/ teachings of Christ

4. As they cross the lake, Jesus comments, **"Be careful, be on your guard against the yeast of the Pharisees and Sadducees."** What do you imagine the disciples' discussion was like after that?

   Focused on bread - food

5. What is the point of Jesus' series of questions to his disciples (verses 8-11)? *Redirect their thoughts + to warn them against false teaching*

6. When they finally get their minds off physical bread, what do the disciples understand?

   guard against teachings of Pharisees + Sadducees

Note: The Pharisees were highly legalistic, concerned with ritual purity and ritual defilement. The Sadducees were primarily political in their religious concerns, and represented the powerful wealthy group of Jews.

7. How can you avoid the attitudes of the Pharisees and Sadducees today? *keep focused on JESUS ready to do his will*

READ MATTHEW 16:13-20

8. Locate Caesarea Philippi on the map on page 75. Now that Jesus and his disciples are alone in this remote place, he puts two questions to them. What do they need to have in order to answer the first question? *information about what people are saying about him*

How would you answer Jesus' question today, "Who do people say I am?"

9. What does the second question demand beyond information (verses 15)? *faith*

What do you think you would have answered if you were one of the twelve disciples? Why?

10. What, do you think, does Simon Peter's answer mean to him and to the rest of the disciples? *recognized Jesus as Messiah*

Note: Some think the disciples must have discussed this question among themselves and that in one sense, Peter is speaking as the foreman of the jury.

11. Put in your own words all the things Jesus says in answer to Peter's declaration (verses 17-20).

You are blessed b/c of your faith You will be the head of my church & draw all men to me

Note: *Rabbis used the terms **binding** and **loosing** to mean* ***forbidding*** *and **permitting**. This seems to foretell Peter's role as leader in the early church in Jerusalem. Jesus calls **Simon** by his family name and then by **Peter**, his nickname which means **rock**. Peter's confession of who Jesus is makes him the first stone in the church. Read his letter (1 Peter 2:4-6) to see the way in which each believer becomes a living stone in the church.*

Note: *Acts 2 and 10 record how Peter was instrumental in unlocking the gates of heaven, or the door of faith, for the Jews and for the Gentiles.*

12. Why can the power of evil and death never conquer the church? *b/c God & his gift of eternal life are more omnipotent.*

13. Why do you think Jesus warns the disciples not to tell anyone he is the Christ (verse 20)? *not right time - had to happen in God's time - Jesus still had work to do*

READ MATTHEW 16:21-23

14. Why do you think that Jesus waits until the disciples are sure of his identity before he gives them the information about his suffering, death and resurrection (verse 21)? *to be sure of their faith & loyalty*

Instead of this announcement, what do you think Peter anticipated happening next?

15. In what way is Peter's attitude a hindrance and a temptation to Jesus at this point?

bitter cup

How can you avoid Peter's mistake of having, not God's point of view, but men's?

READ MATTHEW 16:24-28 IN SEVERAL TRANSLATIONS

16. Put Jesus' statements and questions in verses 24-26 into your own words.

*Note: In verse 26, the NIV uses **life** or **soul** in both questions and the NEB uses **true self.***

17. Jesus gives qualifications for *anyone* who will follow him. What does it mean for you to:
   deny yourself?

   take up your cross?

   follow Jesus?

*Note: The **cross** in that culture was the instrument of death.*

SUMMARY

1. Why was it difficult for the disciples to reconcile what they expected to happen, with Jesus' prediction of his suffering and death?

2. What do you learn from the disciples' experience to help you recognize that God's loving plan for us is not incompatible with suffering?

PRAYER

Lord, you warned your disciples about the teaching of the Pharisees and Sadducees and their way of looking at things. Was it because we must adjust to your way—not of success and power, but of suffering and sacrifice? Lord, help us also to understand! For your glory, Amen.

CHART

What title will you give this chapter on the chart on page 77?

CONCLUSION *to* MATTHEW 1—16

From the beginning of his Gospel, Matthew has one underlying theme—Jesus is the Messiah! This first section of his Gospel emphasizes:

- that Old Testament prophecies about the Messiah (Christ) are fulfilled in the birth and life of Jesus Christ.

- Jesus' definitions of the requirements and rewards of the *kingdom of heaven.*

- Jesus' long teaching sections that describe what his disciples are *to be and to do.*

- the growing conflict between Jesus and the Pharisees, and the Sadducees.

- Jesus' travels and ministry in Gentile territory.

- Jesus' prediction of his death and the requirements for being his disciple.

Look at the chart on page 76-77. Review the book through chapter 16 by reading the titles you have given the chapter divisions.

The Gospel of Matthew reaches a decisive point as Jesus asks his disciples to answer the question, **"*Who do you say I am?*"** Many, from Herod in his palace to the distraught Canaanite mother near Tyre, were concerned with this question. Matthew intends his readers to confront this question and come to a conclusion based on the evidence of Jesus' actions, claims, and teachings.

From what you have discovered in Matthew 1—16, what evidence do you have to help you decide who Jesus is and what his authority is in your life?

Book 2 of the study guide on the Gospel of Matthew has thirteen discussions on Chapters 17—28, covering the events leading up to and including the death and resurrection of Jesus Christ.

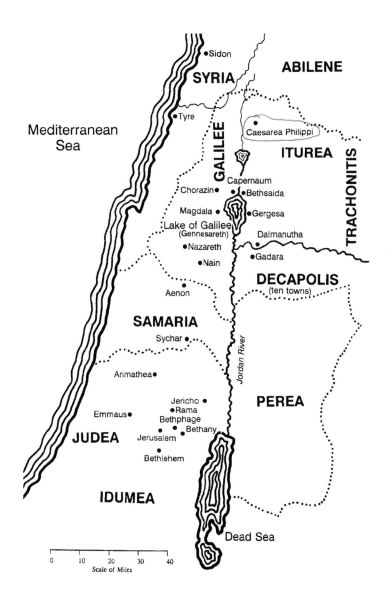

Sidon

SYRIA

ABILENE

Tyre

Mediterranean
Sea

GALILEE

Caesarea Philippi

ITUREA

TRACHONITIS

Capernaum

Chorazin

Bethsaida

Magdala

Gergesa

Lake of Galilee
(Gennesareth)

Dalmanutha

Nazareth

Gadara

Nain

DECAPOLIS
(ten towns)

Aenon

SAMARIA

Sychar

Jordan River

Arimathea

Jericho

PEREA

Rama

Emmaus

Bethphage

Bethany

JUDEA

Jerusalem

Bethlehem

IDUMEA

Dead Sea

0   10   20   30   40
Scale of Miles

CHART OF THE GOSPEL OF MATTHEW

Chapter Title	Event	Place	Time Frame	Instructions:
1		Judea	30 years	Note the geographical movements of Jesus, and of his disciples; the time span involved in segments of the book; significant events; arrangement of material by teaching segments and narrative
2		Egypt → Nazareth		
3		Wilderness		
4	Temptations	Wilderness of Judea		
5	Sermon on the Mount	Galilee		
6				
7				
8				
9			2½ to 3 years	
10	Calling and Instruction of the Twelve			
11				
12	Teaching in Parables			
13				
14	5,000 fed			

Fill in the chart. Make your own chapter titles. Give more details of significant events, and the content of teaching sections.

Chapter	Event	Territory
15	4,000 fed	Gentile Territory
16	"You are the Christ, the Son of the living God"	
17	Transfiguration	Galilee
18	Teaching	Judea beyond Jordan
19		
20		
21	Entry into Jerusalem	Jerusalem
22	Teaching in the Temple	
23		
24	Signs of the End / Teaching His Disciples	
25	Parables	
26	Last Supper / Gethsemane	
27	Trials before Caiaphas and Pilate	
28	Resurrection	Galilee

one week

WHAT SHOULD OUR GROUP STUDY NEXT?

We recommend the Gospel of Mark, the fast paced narrative of Jesus' life, as the first book for people new to Bible study. Follow this with the Book of Acts to see what happens to the people introduced in Mark. Then in Genesis discover the beginnings of the world and find the answers to the big questions of where we came from and why we are here.

Our repertoire of guides allows great flexibility. For groups starting with *Lenten Studies*, *They Met Jesus* is a good sequel.

LEVEL 101: little or no previous Bible study experience
Mark *(recommended first unit of study)* or The Book of Mark *(Simplified English)*

Acts, Books 1 and 2
Genesis, Books 1 and 2
Psalms/Proverbs
Topical Studies
Conversations With Jesus
Lenten Studies
Foundations for Faith
Character Studies
They Met Jesus

> **Sequence for groups reaching people from non-Christian cultures**
> Foundations for Faith
> Genesis, Books 1 and 2
> Mark, Discover Jesus *or* The Book of Mark *(Simplified English)*

LEVEL 201: some experience in Bible study (after 3-4 Level 101 books)

John, Books 1 and 2	Treasures
Romans	Relationships
I John/James	Servants of the Lord
1 Corinthians	Change
2 Corinthians	Work – God's Gift
Philippians	Celebrate
Colossians	*Character Studies*
Topical Studies	Four Men of God
Prayer	Lifestyles of Faith, Books 1 and 2

LEVEL 301: More experienced in Bible study

Matthew, Books 1 and 2	*Topical Studies*
Galatians & Philemon	Set Free
1 and 2 Peter	*Character Studies*
Hebrews	David
1 and 2 Thessalonians, 2 & 3 John	Moses
Isaiah	**Biweekly or Monthly Groups may use topical studies or character studies.
Ephesians	

ABOUT NEIGHBORHOOD BIBLE STUDIES

Neighborhood Bible Studies, Inc. is a leader in the field of small group Bible studies. Since 1960, NBS has pioneered the development of Bible study groups that encourage each member to participate in the leadership of the discussion.

The Mission of Neighborhood Bible Studies is to mobilize Christians to facilitate group discussions with spiritual seekers so they can find God as revealed in the bible.

The Vision of Neighborhood Bible Studies is for Christians all over the world inviting people into small groups to question, discover and grow in their relationship with God.

Publication in more than 20 languages indicates the versatility of NBS cross culturally. NBS **methods and materials** are used around the world to:

> Equip individuals for facilitating discovery Bible studies
> Serve as a resource to the church

Skilled NBS personnel provide consultation by telephone or e-mail. In some areas, they conduct workshops and seminars to train individuals, clergy, and laity in how to establish small group Bible studies in neighborhoods, churches, workplaces and specialized facilities. **Call 1–800–369–0307 to inquire about consultation or training.**

ABOUT THE FOUNDERS

Marilyn Kunz and Catherine Schell, authors of many of the NBS guides, founded Neighborhood Bible Studies and directed its work for thirty-one years. Currently other authors contribute to the series.

The cost of your study guide has been subsidized by faithful people who give generously to NBS. For more information, visit our web site: www.neighborhoodbiblestudy.org   *1–800–369–0307*

COMPLETE LISTING OF NBS STUDY GUIDES

Getting Started
How to Start a Q Place

Bible Book Studies
Genesis, Book 1 *Begin with God*
Genesis, Book 2 *Discover Your Roots*
Psalms & Proverbs *Journals of Wisdom*
Isaiah *God's Help Is on the Way*
Matthew, Book 1 *God's Promise Kept*
Matthew, Book 2 *God's Purpose Fulfilled*
Mark *Discover Jesus*
Luke *Good News and Great Joy*
John, Book 1 *Explore Faith and Understand Life*
John, Book 2 *Believe and Live*
Acts, Book 1 *The Holy Spirit Transforms Lives*
Acts, Book 2 *Amazing Journeys with God*
Romans *A Reasoned Faith*
1 Corinthians *Finding Answers to Life's Questions*
2 Corinthians *The Power of Weakness*
Galatians & Philemon *Fully Accepted by God*
Ephesians *Living in God's Family*
Philippians *A Message of Encouragement*
Colossians *Staying Focused on Truth*
1 & 2 Thessalonians, 2 & 3 John, Jude *The Coming of the LORD*
Hebrews *Access to God*
1 & 2 Peter *Strength Amidst Stress*
1 John & James *Faith that Lives*

Topical Studies
Celebrate *Reasons for Hurrahs*
Conversations with Jesus *Getting to Know Him*
Change *Facing the Unexpected*
Foundations for Faith *The Basics for Knowing God*
Lenten Studies *Life Defeats Death*
Prayer *Communicating with God*
Relationships *Connect to Others: God's Plan*
Servants of the LORD *Embrace God's Agenda*
Set Free *Leaving Negative Emotions Behind*
Treasures *Discover God's Riches*
Work – God's Gift *Life-Changing Choices*

Character Studies
Four Men of God *Unlikely Leaders*
Lifestyles of Faith, Book One *Choosing to Trust God*
Lifestyles of Faith, Book Two *Choosing to Obey God*
They Met Jesus *Life-Changing Encounters*
David *Passions Pursued*
Moses *Learning to Lead*

Simplified English
The Book of Mark *The Story of Jesus*